My Life in Little Pieces

ISBN #: 978-1-387-68278-2

"I don't exist without writing."

-Jewel Kilcher

A note from my heart:

Thank you so much for taking
the time to read this. By
opening this book, you are
taking a look inside my soul.
You have no idea how much
that means.

Wow. I can't believe this book is finally published. I have been working on the content for several years, and I finally feel that it's ready for the world to read. I started this back when I was just an innocent high school girl with a hunger for love, a wild heart, and dreams as big as the sky. Through my free spirited teenage years and the transition into real adulthood, I have experienced many phases of life, and just now have I really begun to figure out who I am as a human, a woman, and a writer.

The only way I have ever been able to express my truest, most authentically raw feelings has been through writing poetry and song lyrics, and I will tell you why: Words never change, they are black and white, and you can't take them back. Once the emotions of my core are down on paper, there they remain. They are off my chest, out of my brain, and in the hands of the universe. My words are there to be read, to be reflected on, and to be learnt from. These poetic pages make up all the little pieces of my life, the thirty-one years of who I am today.

This book has been my greatest accomplishment yet, a fresh, from the soul performance of my realest, unfiltered being, and there is no way this vision would have come to life without the inspiration of so many people. More than anything, I want to express my deepest gratitude to my mother and father for always being my biggest fans. Thank you, Mom and Dad, for molding me into the strong, independent, and assertive person I am today. You've always encouraged me to follow my dreams, and I did. Next, an immense thank you goes to my sister and best friend, Jacy. I have always looked up to you, and I would be lost in this huge world without you. You have taught me to be fierce and brave in ways I never knew I could be - I'm so lucky to have you in my corner. To my whole family (blood or not), we may not have it all together, but together, we have always had it all. My love for you is endless. I also want to thank all the friends and strangers who have come and gone, all the mentors who I have admired and respected, and all the boys and men who have both loved me and hurt me. You all have taught me what it means to grow, what it means to have courage, how to toughen my heart and strengthen my being, and how to truly love myself from the inside out.

     To all the people who believed in me, and to the ones who couldn't wait to see me fall, this one's for you.

With peace and love,
Holly

A Collection of Poetry & Lyrics

By

Holly Amber Wolti

Colors

And when I see him, I see red
Not the shade that makes you mad
But makes your heart bleed instead

And I still remember every word that we said
And the color of the moon shining on that bed

It was screaming yellow
But all I heard was Red

A Nine to Fiver

His hands are so hardworking
Calloused to the touch
His mind is so much stronger
Than anything I've ever loved

He doesn't even need to move
And eyes are all on him
People beg to hear him laugh
A gentle antonym

A drinker on the weekends
He likes his glass so strong
He loves it more than me sometimes
The scotch can do no wrong

But I play my role, I do my part
I wake at six
My morning start
And we try so hard, we pay the bills
We never miss our night time thrills

But I love it when he's sober
When he's everything I need
'Til Friday becomes Sunday
And I start to beg and plead

And Monday comes, it always does
Steals away his final buzz
He'll love me hard, he'll never stop
'Til Friday night at 5 o'clock

October

There's something 'bout October
And the way the cold wind blows
It's a thought I can't get over
The what ifs and who knows

There's something in the air
The way it hits my skin
The way he looked in our first glance
Before innocence was sin

There's something in that sky
And the burnt leaves on the ground
The way I tried to hide the truth
Of the yearning so profound

But these feelings started to fade
When I become more sober
So is it really him I miss
Or is it just last October

Blue

It was right around 10:30
I was lonely, buzzed, and cold
I saw him in the corner
My eyes caught his, strong and bold

I can't remember what was said
Or how I even caught his name
But a shot and three drinks later
We were lost inside the game

And I don't know how we got there
If I was sad or just worn out
But I hoped that when he left that bar
I'd be what he thought about

A stranger then, less stranger now
But I still think about that night somehow
I guess some memories they never fade
Of a blurry night, with secrets made

And we still talk, we say hello
We joke about that winter coat
And it's funny how I wish I knew
If he was only lonely, drunk, or blue

Singing

I want to engrave my poetry
Into the ground
And tattoo my love
To your skin
I want to look at the world
From top to bottom
And swallow my words
So I can sing them to you
Again and again

Show Me Off

I guess what I'm trying to say is
My words are sharp, ready to break your skin
And marry your blood
Float through your body
Up a purple throat
To the harbor of your mouth

I want you to sing my poetry so loud
'Cause my teeth are too anxious to talk
And yours is the only voice I trust enough
To show me off

See, my tongue is a pale skinned infant
Speaking nothing but the absence of words
And all I have is this pen
Which is sweating
'Cause it knows you are afraid

Insecurity gnaws hard on my bones
But I want so badly for the world to know how I feel
So I need to borrow you, love
And your perfectly shaped lips
To save me
And tell my story tonight

People in Cars

Soaring through the greatest heights
Shooting through white dreams
Numb to all sounds now
Except the way you said I love you too

I wonder if you are somewhere below me
Driving, driving, driving away
To your new life
The one you wanted
Replaying our last kiss
Reliving our first time
In your mind

I'm so high above you
Yet I feel two inches small
Oh I'm sure going to need you
When my fears come visit me tonight

But on this plane, I'm flying
Away from my sorrow
But I'll be back at some point
And so will you

Trying

The days drag on
Like a rusty freight train
You wonder when it will slow down
And stop

And I move on
Through short days and long nights
And I wear these jeans quite often
Because they mean something

I still get nervous when it's dark
But I try to make my way
Between alarm clocks
And late night calls

And I still give all I can
With milky white thighs and little wrists
Because I know for sure if you were here
You'd tell me to never give up

In Strawberry Fields

Today
A branch scraped the bottom of my foot
Slicing my skin
Invisible blood came out

You said it doesn't hurt
I would be okay, so
I smiled chasing after you

Crunch!
I looked, and the leaves winked at me
They could sense it too
And in that very moment
I loved you

Mermaid

Always being pulled under
Like an anchor to the ground
Weighted to the ocean floor
My ears are deaf to any sound

Secluded in this world
I created of my own
I take pride in the solace
I find when I'm alone

I could swim up to the land
Break the water with my hands
But they are too content
Six miles from the sand

If I walked along the stretch of earth
I've seen only in my dreams
Confusion might prove
It really isn't what it seems

Devoured by embarrassment
I'll swan dive in again
Surrounded in the waves
Of my hidden sea within

Freezing Time

I want to photograph your back
Every freckle
Every imperfection
Perfect to me

I want to memorize your muscles
And the taste of your lips
And borrow your scent
To wear to bed tonight

I want to kiss your face and never stop
I want to kiss your mouth and never stop
Can I kiss your hands and never stop

December

Show me that your heart is still designed
To love me
And I'll show you
That Christmas bulbs still dangle
From the strings of my mind

And I'll promise that every star in the sky
Still has your name on it
And the man in the moon above my bed
Still has green eyes

Show me that snowfalls make you miss me
And that your heart still stops at red lights
Because you remember the way I looked
In downtown traffic

Maybe it's my name
Or just this time of year
But this city has got the best of me again,
Now it's the 24th, so where can you be found

For You

Take me for a summer walk
Over a careless stream
Across a broken bridge
We're both a little too scared to walk across

I'll go first and pretend I'm brave
Make believe there's no sweat on my shoulders
I'll act like I have no fear
For you

Comfortable

So clever are you, my love
To leave behind a memory of me
And my hair
Tangled, loose, comfortable

There is a story
On your nightstand
And you shall reminisce some autumn eve
And maybe you will reach for me

Laying where I loved you
Dreaming where we kissed
Crave to see my silhouette
In the shadow on your wall

Oh, a long time it will be
Until you touch that memory again
Of my hair
Tangled, loose, comfortable

California

Sing to me, beautiful bird
Hum the sweet, sweet harmony
In my little ear
And I'll fasten up my eyes
Fall into a West Coast trance
Dashing naked into the ocean blue

California, let me make you my home
Can I swing from your sunrays
And swallow your coconuts whole

Little bird, did you sleep in a palm tree
Did you watch all the girls sing their rock 'n roll

Oh, California,
Can I make you my home

Baby Blue

How foolish was I
A child of the sun
To seek simplicity
On this complex earth

How crazy were you
My baby blue
To wrap your love in a gift box
And surprise me

Your broke your own rules
Ripping through the seams
Giving into my depth
Falling in love
Proving love by your tears

Solitude now
You are my only friend
Let's share this night and pray him back

My baby blue is gone
I wonder if he's all alone

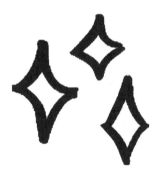

A Small Town Goodbye

When we're driving in your car at night
Constellations paint the sky so bright
I don't see a soul in sight
It's only you and me
How you wanted it to be

And if I could freeze this time with you
I would hold your hand forever
And I'd stop to kiss your eyelids
My life could not be better

The smell of your skin is enough to show
The reasons why your green eyes glow
Ten thousands poets will never know
The words to say when it's time to go

The Perfect Face

When you look at me and see
The girl they wanted me to be
Are you still proud
Am I too loud
Am I too free

You listen to my voice, and
Then you analyze my poise
Have I got it down
In this big crowd
Can you still see me

Beneath this hat of lace
And flawless, faultless grace
My fears resound
They think they've found
The perfect face

Well, I know it's not my place
But I ponder, just in case
Can I make a sound
Is that allowed
Would they be disgraced

A Requiem for Autumn

She stings me in the morning
Her sharp wind cuts my face
I wonder where the summer went
But for her, it's not a race

She breaks and cracks beneath my feet
Her leaves, they just keep falling
She thinks she's losing all her strength, and
She knows that winter's calling

Her name is Autumn, gorgeous gold
Still young at heart, but feels so old
When all her reds have turned to brown
Her skin is shedding to the ground

I'm there to catch it, if I can
So I reach out my little hand
I hold onto her until she's gone
While Winter sings the saddest song

A Maybe Poem

Maybe I'm lost in a world with so much to think about
A universe bigger than I could ever dream about
Do I care more than I should
Maybe I don't care enough
Maybe I'm just a free spirit with too much to love

Maybe I'm trying too hard
Maybe I don't know my place
I just want to save it all
The entire human race
Maybe I need a step back
A cool gentle breath
Fade away quietly from the busy streets of stress

But this life is a platform
We want to rise to the top
Maybe that's our biggest problem
And we all need to stop
Well, one thing's for sure
If there's anything I know
It's that we need to slow down
Watch the sun glow

I think we're moving way too fast
Maybe we're missing out on life
We're spending all our time asking if we've got it right
This breathtaking world can be too much to take, and
Maybe sometimes honest hands just need a break

Small Talk

The summer sun starts melting down
Over that busy little bar in town
Secrets filling up the air
She wonders how the night will end
With rumors floating friend to friend
Her skin is burning from their stare

Laughs it off, it's nothing new
She's used to it, and he is too
She won't let them know she cares
So she just keeps her shoulders tall
And she just lets her blonde hair fall
It's better when she's unaware

Oh, she fascinates them as she moves
Through crowds of faces, old and new
Making small talk here and there
She yells, another round for my new friends
We don't even care how much we spend
See, we all have broken hearts to mend
You know that's why we're here

A few more shots, a few less feelings
Tonight tequila's doing all healing
This girl could really use a prayer
She bites her straw, hell bent on drinking
It keeps her from doing too much thinking
As she falls back into her chair

Now it's just about that closing time
She walks out the door into the night
Hanging memories on the streetlights
But tonight she won't go home

She'll end up where she's meant to be
Or maybe where she'd rather be
But she makes sure she's not alone

Hopeful Girl

I don't care what it takes
I'd like a faultless world
They say that can't exist
And I'm just a hopeful girl
But hopeful girls, they've seen the most
Their hearts have felt real pain, and
They're the ones who sing the loudest
Under pouring acid rains

But I don't care how much it burns
I'm gonna dance on every star
I want to swallow up their fire, and
Let their flames engrave a scar
They used to seem so small, I laugh
Each tiny blazing tear, but
Now a million specks of glowing light
Are dripping starlight in my hair

This is where I'll live, I think
To the constellations, I'll exclaim
I'll never judge a stranger
'Cause up here, we shine the same
See, the Earth just seems too shallow now
For hopeful girls like me, and
I'd rather bathe in waves of bright red freedom
Than in a superficial sea

Red Lipstick at a Vintage Bar

In borrowed heels, her Mama's dress
She walks to the bar alone
One last spray of cheap perfume
Trickles down her collar bone

Walks up the stairs, into the room
And she always looks the same
Her hands clenched behind her skinny back
Her troubled little frame

Well no one said her life was easy
But they've never stopped to ask
Where is it she comes from
Is she ever going back

Red lipstick on her restless smile, and
You can see it in her wrists
Pulsing faster as she finds him
Drinking whiskey with a twist

He's tried before to save her
To mend her injured heart
Still he swears he'll never quite give up
You know he's loved her from the start

Her hidden scars that no one sees
Warm blood that no one feels
He knows her soul's gorgeous mess
He knows her pain is real

Fastened eyes across the room
The band plays a tune so blue
With shivered lips she mouths the words

Boy, this song was made for me and you

Her fingers start to tremble now
And she reaches for his hands
She prays that he won't let her down
For this is her first dance

She'd never trust a man before
Enough to hold her in his arms
But something in his deep green eyes
Ignites a vicious charm

He spins and twirls and lifts her up
He knows she's his for sure
But something stops, she pulls away
And she rushes to the door

Well no one said her life was easy
But they never stop to ask
Where is it she's going to
Is she ever coming back

You Did

I've risked the flames, I've cried the rain
Watched your heart bleed, broke through your chains
I've held you close, pushed you away
Longing to hear you say you'd stay
And you did

Like a winter's night, I tore through your skin
Sewed you up, to rip through again
Made you show me who you really are
Made you tell me about all your scars
And you did

But you were getting close, so I ran fast
I thought a love this rich could never last
How could someone want my vagrant soul
Like a wild angel, soaring out of control
But you did

You threw the bricks right through my walls
You carved, and cut, fought through them all
You stole my heart, you cleaned me up
You showed me I was worth your love
Yes, you did

You kissed my eyes, you touched my hair
You agreed with me that life's not fair
You said if we have each other, that's all we need
So you took my hand, you took the lead
You did

Now here I am, I wonder why
I played those games, I made you cry
Cause I've never known a love so strong

I know it now, I knew it all along

And I lay in bed, I stare at your face
Your skin, your breath, my saving grace
Don't ever leave, into your ear
Begging God, those words you'd hear
And you did

Red Canoe

Young love sweating in a red canoe
You say, look at that sky
But all I see is you
Tan skin pulsing, I think I see your heart
I want to swallow it whole
So we'll never have to part

And I'm sure that this is magic
'Cause it really can't be real
You're seeing parts of me I promised
I'd never quite reveal
But there's something 'bout that shimmer
From the sun down to the lake
And I'm thinking back to when I said
You were my best mistake

Now you're giving me that same old look
I've seen a billion times before
I've memorized your smile, and
I've never been so sure
I laugh, sometimes the best things
Just can't be foreseen
Gotta let your heart outweigh your head
You know just what I mean

You pause before you answer
You just stare at me so hard
Then you lean right in to kiss me
You love catching me off guard
You tell me just to listen; you swear these words are true
You say, No one's ever loved you girl, the way that I sure
do

Now we're back at shore, it's later now
The onyx sky has lost its blue
My mind's repeating what you said
The way you looked in that canoe
You notice that I'm drifting off
I think you're drifting too
You say look up at the stars, my love
But all I see is you

Dream

Everyone had diamond earrings
And a bright gold wedding band
She had worn out sneakers
And a night-shift working man
The old cross her Daddy gave her
Sat securely on her chest
She held it while she prayed at night
Asking God for a rest

She swept the floors, she made the beds
She kept her little babies fed
He brought home fifty bucks a week
But she never had bad words to speak
'Cause she knew there must be more out there
Wild wind to tangle up their hair
So she'd dream

When the kids grew up and went to school
She went out to make some money too
Her paycheck wasn't very much
She never really had great luck
But she remembered what her momma said
Pretty girl don't ever lose your head
It's a cold world out there, ya know
So don't ever let the good ones go
Hold on tightly to that man of yours
Run your fingers through your babies' curls
And dream

Now they're both in their sixties
Their kids have kids of their own
Their little corner city flat
Is what the both of them call home

He still smiles; he looks her up and down
In her worn out little pink night gown
He says "My sweet lady it's all alright
We've made it through harder nights
I'm right beside you every single day
Close your eyes now, love, it's all okay
So just dream

The Saddest Eclipse

Ever think of what will happen when the sun gives up its
light
Knowing all too well that it's just not worth the fight
When the sky just separates and there's nothing left in sight
'Cause the moon, you know, she always wins
Whether wrong or right

That stubborn moon, the stars will scream
Why can't she understand
She's nothing but a cold dark sphere
Without the sun to hold her hand
And just like that, regret sinks in
But she won't change her mind
Too stubborn to admit she's wrong
Leaving the world below her blind

And a lunar love comes to an end
It hurts worse than she'll make known
But she wants to shine all by herself
Light the sky all on her own
And so it comes, a deep black smoke
Everything just fades
And the sun sits there behind a cloud
Wiping tears off of its face

See, nothing lasts forever
As the sun was taught to learn
But we all need some help from somebody
Or like the moon, we'll crash and burn

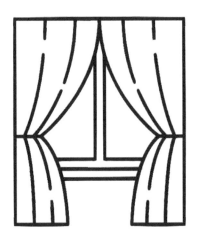

Thursday's Song

Sunrise peaks right at me
Through the window pane
And I squint
Another day already
God I just laid my blonde hair on the bed
I roll my eyes at my own self, grab some faith, get out of
bed
And tell the world it's my turn today

See, I've given up on worry but I worry that I won't worry
enough
Makes sense
My brain is like a riddle
A web you won't get through, but oh-well
I'm luckier than lots of you
I envy all the rest
My reflection's in the mirror, and my towel's falling down,
Yeah I'm blessed

See, it's been a jagged ride, but I've got angels on my side
Laughing 'cause my life's a gorgeous mess
And I let go of the all the stress

The five o'clock traffic tries to rape me of smile yet again,
I just found peace today
So I promise not to let these thirty minutes win
'Cause when I get home, he's waiting there
The bed, the walls, love's everywhere
It's our little land, it's me and him

So I run into the room thanking God for all that's good
And he grins
My work clothes fall away, the day light starts to fade

I touch his skin
We laugh and for the first time I'm myself again

See, it's been a jagged ride, but I've got angels on my side
Laughing 'cause my life's a gorgeous mess
And I let go of all the stress

Fragile Girl

They say she's too outspoken
Other days too shy
They tell her she's not perfect
And to stop the fight to try
They love her face
They hate her back
She keeps it calm
Then she attacks
She's a complicated girl
In a big bewildered world

She has a heart of gold
The softest skin
Long blonde hair
A gentle grin
She tries too hard for everyone
For everything she sees
She fixes all their broken wounds
While hers just bleed and bleed
She's a different kind of girl
In a big bewildered world

She prays at night when she lays down
Nine different angels hear her sound,
Please guard my family
Bless all my friends
And if you think you have the time
Please love me in the end
She's a giver and a selfless girl
In a big bewildered world

She comes off tough
She comes off loud

She comes off confident
Way too proud
And when she cries
They run away
Can't bear to see a fighter
Crumble down to clay
She's a mystery of a girl
In a big bewildered world

So next time that you see her
Remember who she is
She's hiding things you'll never know
She's just a person, still a kid
So before you're quick to judge her
Because you think she's judging you
Take a step back and remember
We're all wishing on that same big moon.

She's trying her best to do what she can
She gives and gives and has demands
She's just a fragile girl
In a convoluted world

Every Piece of Me

It's not just in the outline
Of blue veins below your skin
Or the way I trace them while you sleep
When you're breathing out, then in

It's not only in your shadow
Fixed tall over my head
Or the way I hold so tightly
Onto every word you've ever said

It's more than lakes, and leaves
And sweaty skin
Of summer heat
Or burning tin

It's bigger than the sky, you know
A miscreation, or a crimson snow
It's how we went against the odds of all
That October night, that faultless fall

It's fiercer than the tallest flame
It puts the galaxy at wretched shame
It's hot to touch, with a tender feel
It's bold, alive, so raw, so real

It's the brashness of your arrow
Sharper than I've ever seen
In the way it cuts right through my ribs
Giving you the deepest parts of me

It's in the songs I write
The words I read
The tears I cry

The blood I bleed
My bones, my lips, my hands, my knees
You are every piece of me

Better Than Her

He said it himself, you're better than her
He told me himself when I walked through his door
He gave me himself, when he chose me each time
He felt it, himself, when his hands met my spine

He showed me things that I'd never seen
I believed in the words he just didn't mean
I trusted him with my discolored heart
Cause the way that he moved
It was some form of art

Please stay the night, he asked me each time
He said it himself, I wish you were mine
What a selfish boy, he wanted it all
He loved the addiction
He watched me fall

I believed in his lies, I believed in his eyes
I hated to leave and those drunken goodbyes
And I'd find myself missing that look on his face
But a scandal it was, a dishonest embrace

He tried, but he lied, we ended up hurt
And I wonder what became of my old tee shirt
The one I that wore when it all fell apart
The last time I let that boy near my heart

Please stay the night, he asked me each time
He said it himself, I wish you were mine
What a selfish boy, he wanted it all
He loved the addiction
He watched me fall

Well it ended fast - quicker than it began
What else to expect from such a small man

What a selfish boy, he wanted it all
But I dodged that bullet – a painful close call

Christmas Eve

A voice, a place, a familiar smell
A circumstance I know so well
Uniting eyes over a drinking glass
Tender smiles as people pass

It's the how are you, where have you been
Regretting the time it's been since then
A sudden sadness strikes the heart
Wishing time could stop, and pause to start

Red lips from wine, a buzzing smile
Wow I haven't been here in a while
Glossy bulbs strung on the tree
A laugh, a kiss, a wink at me

Drinks collide, a joyful cheer
The well-known scent of winter beer
Delight for all, ignoring age
Of stockings green, a Christmas sage

The night moves on, we say goodbye
Some they laugh, some start to cry
For loved ones lost, prayers are prayed
Memories had, memories made

Tomorrow it will come so soon
I gaze up at the December moon
I thank the stars for cherished time
For holidays spent with this circle of mine

Waiting on You

Waiting on summer days
Orange mornings and purple nights
A full wine glass after an evening fight
How the lake makes everything all right

Waiting on bright white stars
On boats and waves and sweating hearts
With hopes to catch a glimpse of Mars
And drinks on docks instead of bars

Waiting on sandy feet
A place where we all will meet
To laugh and sing and cheers to this
A place I'll go to reminisce

Waiting on you
On changes made and warmer skies
On more hellos and less goodbyes
On giving this an honest try
Waiting on you

Take Me Back

I don't know what it was about that night
Or the night soon after that
All I know is I'm here wishing, putting up a fight
Begging God to take me back

It's funny when you're lost inside a moment
How it goes by so damn fast
No way to stop and freeze and just hold it
What will soon become your past

So take me back, to when I didn't have a care
Take me back, to pick up lines and tangled hair
When the consequence ahead
Didn't stand a chance to stop us both
If you could take me back, take back, take me back
Would you say no

Suddenly the days were passing slowly
Until I realized what we both already knew
That you were just inspired, just excited
By the touch of someone else, something new

'Cause nothing shines forever, the shimmer fades away
You've moved on and on and on again
While I'm hanging on to words I didn't say

So take me back, to when I didn't have a care
Take me back, to pick up lines and tangled hair
When the consequence ahead
Didn't stand a chance to stop us both
If you could take me back, take back, take me back
Would you say no

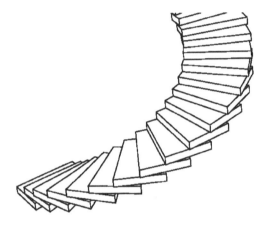

Should've Left My Heart at the Door

I drive up to your house, a little past eleven
Thinking this could burn like hell
For a moment's worth of heaven
And the pain that this is gonna cause
But here I go, I clench my fists
Tonight I'm yours

So I park my car across the street
I know you're waiting there for me
I walk right in, like I own the place
And when I see your face

I realize - I should've left my heart the door
Cause this pounding in my chest, it's too hard to ignore
My legs go numb when you touch my skin
Disappointed in myself that I'm here again
And as the moon light beams through your window to the
floor
I look into your eyes, and I realize
I should've left my heart at the door

We play pretend like this ain't even wrong
For a little while longer, now I'm acting like I'm strong
Cause I just don't want to have to miss you yet
You pull me in, touch my hair, and for a second I forget

I should've left my heart at the door
Cause this pounding in my chest, it's too hard to ignore
My legs go numb when you touch my skin
Disappointed in myself that I'm here again
And as the moon light beams through your window to the
floor
I look into your eyes and I realize

I should've left my heart at the door

Now it's getting late, guess we've gotta say goodbye
But I stop and wait, hoping you ask me to stay the night
But I know things like that just can't happen anymore
So one last kiss, grab my coat, down the stairs
Take a breath, and now I'm sure

I should've left my heart at the door
Cause this pounding in my chest, it's too hard to ignore
My legs go numb when you touch my skin
Disappointed in myself that I'm here again
And as the moon light beams through your window to the
floor
I look into your eyes and I realize
I should've left my heart at the door

Wishing You Were Mine

She's beautiful, she knows just how to walk
And she's careful, she knows when to stop
If she's giving too much, not taking enough
She knows just how to keep you in line
But what she doesn't know is how to stop you
From wishing you were mine

Like a picture, she knows just how to pose
She's flawless, her hair, her painted toes
She always shows up, she's right by your side
Wherever you go, she's along for the ride
But what she doesn't know is how to stop you
From wishing you were mine

She puts you on display for the world to feel her love
The one she knows so well you're not deserving of
Her heart has felt some pain
It's broken once or twice
But like I've always been to you
You're her strongest vice

And I can't understand, she's everything and more
Yeah you're such a spoiled man, of that we all are sure
But still she wishes she could stop you
From wishing I was her

Sting

Looking back I thought I'd never be here
Pen in hand, writing him this song
I feel my face and I just can't believe it
Not a single tear, my God it's been so long

I've played it in my head a thousand times
I've practiced all those perfect miss-you lines
What I'd tell him if the moment ever came
But there I stood, there he was, and all that I could say is

Why doesn't it hurt
Why doesn't it sting
How come I'm not crying, I'm still trying
But I don't feel a thing
I guess it's been too long
He never was the one
Maybe all his lying and all that fighting
Made my naïve heart go numb

And now I really don't know why I even went there
To his house to visit his new life
But all those drinks and his familiar laughter
Made me start to question wrong from right

So I stayed with him, let him try again
He convinced me I should just give in
I prayed that when the morning came
I would feel something for him, so

Why doesn't it hurt
Why doesn't it sting
How come I'm not crying, I'm still trying
But I don't feel a thing

I guess it's been too long
He never was the one
Maybe all his lying and all that fighting
Made my naive heart go numb

Pray

I've wanted all of this since I was just a child
A world where everybody gets along
Where the birds, flowers, and all of the forest
Live together, whispering a honeyed song

I want to breathe in all the good, exhale all the hate
Have no more war, no more fear, but I don't wanna wait
Want it now, begged for it then, I just want us to all be
friends
And I don't know what else I can do
So I pray

I pray for peace, I pray for light
I pray we all learn wrong from right
For all the things I wanted as a little girl
I pray for you, I pray for me
I pray that everyone will see
That love trumps fear every single time
Just listen to this voice of mine

I pray for him, I pray for me
And for the homeless on the street
I write for her, I sing for them
All I ask is when
This old world will bleed more love than blood
I'm asking God above

That we can breathe in all the good, exhale all the hate
Have no more war, no more fear, no we don't want to wait
We want it now, begged for it then, we just all want to be
friends
And we don't know what else we can do
So we pray

Whiskey

I've tried calling you all night, but you don't care
I know just where you are, I know who's there
I know that smell, I know that place
I know the look that's on your face
When you see my number calling every hour

I bet you're leaning back on that old bar stool
Blowing smoke into the air the way you do
A fearless flicker in your heart
A feeling you can only get
From the Bourbon or the Tennessee
You never get that drunk on me
I wish you loved me like the Whiskey

You see my name and you just press ignore
Can't let me ruin your good time, I'm sure
It's half past twelve, it's getting late
I'm so tired but I sit and wait
I feel like I don't even know you anymore
And I'm stuck here staring at the door

Wish I could turn you on the way it does
Touch your lips, give you that buzz
Be the reason you stay out all night
Let me be the fire in your eyes
Let me be the reason for your lies

A few more shots and now you're getting stronger
I'm lying here wondering how much longer
I don't think I can take much more of this

I bet you're leaning back on that old bar stool
Blowing smoke into the air the way you do

A fearless flicker in your heart
A feeling you can only get
From the Bourbon or the Tennessee
You never get that drunk on me
I wish you loved me like the Whiskey

I wish I could make you miss me
I wish you loved me like the Whiskey

Proud

The switch of a light, wrong versus right
The touch of your hand, I don't give a damn
The smell of the rain, it drives me insane
I feel like a fool, and you're keeping your cool

The spark of the pain, the sting of the change
A much different place, a much different face
The sound of your voice, I'm stuck with a choice
I know I can't make, you know I could break

A couple drinks more, I stare at the door
I don't want to leave, I just want to breathe
Holding onto the night, avoiding the fight
I don't say a word, I don't want to hurt

We turn up the sound, your shirt on the ground
You get lost in this, I get lost in your kiss
The music is loud, you're feeling so proud
You pulled this one off, you're not getting caught

Your eyes are so kind, even when you lie
Your posture is bold, but your heart is so cold
I know all of this, but I just can't resist
And I feel like a fool, 'cause you're keeping your cool

Wings

Every time those words slip off your tongue
You think they'll crush me
Hurt me
Break me
But instead they take me
Make me
Strong
Better
They ignite the flame inside my soul
They pump the blood into my heart
They reinforce my wings
They color my soul
Red
Yellow
Gold
They remind me who I am
So
That the more you tell me I won't get there
The further I will fly

Holidays

I want your holidays
I want your dreams
I want all the things
She gets to see

I want your hands
I want your fists
Your morning breath
Your goodnight kiss

I want your teeth
To speak to me
Your chocolate eyes to blink at me

I want your warmness when it's cold
And I'll give you my waist to hold
I want your fears
I want your doubts
To teach me what you're all about

To be so much more than what we are
To be the one you lay with under stars
To know all the places that you've been
To just be so much more than this
I want to know the story of your scars

A Criminal Love

Careless of failure
Two reckless fools
With eyes burning brighter
Than the Tennessee moon

Making up words
To make believe songs
Staying out late
Doing everything wrong

A girl and a boy
Who don't give a damn
Caught up in the danger
Of a cursed lover's scam

Let Me

I'd be so much better at loving you
Baby can't you see
I'd never hold you back
From what you want to do
I'd let your heart be free
From anything that weighs you down
I'd always be around
To pick you up when you need
So baby just let me

Bullet

You say you've had enough of that old life
One day soon you're gonna make me your wife
But we both know that's all for show, and so it goes
And so it goes

You'll get tired of me again soon enough
Remind me that I'm just too hard to love
Make me feel like it's all my fault
Throw it in my face, you just can't stop
You choose me last when push comes down to shove

Each time you do it, you do it
Don't you know that we're both running
From that same old bullet, bullet
Just gotta get me through it, through it
So I can sleep through the noise and the heat
Of your bullet

But then you realize that this just ain't fair
The game's getting old
And it's way too much to bear
You see what it's doing to my bruised up heart
You're watching me literally fall apart
You don't give a damn 'til my hands are in the air

One day soon I'll rise above
I'll fly like a jet plane away from your love
I'll be so far away even if you wanted to do it
You could try like hell but the truth is
You'd never reach me with your bullet

Each time you do it, you do it
Don't you know that we're both running

From that same old bullet, bullet
Just gotta get me through it, through it
So I can sleep through the noise and the heat
Of your bullet

Speechless

Got a history with you but they don't know
Anger and resentment I can't show
Lots of good times, lots of laughs
Lots of could have's and should have's
But I can't just sit around in sorrow, so I'll go

Can't show my face around here anymore
I know my place, I know it's out the door
And I can't help but feel alone
But looking back, I should have known
You took advantage of my innocence, so pure

All the things you've done, the games you always won
I wonder if you hurt me just for fun
Too good to be true, but the lies looked good on you
You held so tightly to your smoking gun

Now it's been so long since you've tried
But it ain't been long since I've cried
I guess that I should finally move on
The secrets and the shame, the inevitable blame
I'll take the fall for you, I'll be strong

I used to think that I was just a test
Another pretty girl you wanted like the rest
Oh I've tried to find the words, but I can't cause I'm a mess
Never thought you being gone would leave me speechless

Now it's been so long since you've tried
But it ain't been long since I've cried
I guess that I should finally move on
The secrets and the shame, the inevitable blame
I'll take the fall for you, I'll be strong

NOTES

NOTES

NOTES

NOTES

NOTES

NOTES

NOTES

NOTES